# STU DUVAL

# RAT
# ISLAND

Published by Pearson Education Limited, Edinburgh Gate, Harlow, Essex, CM20 2JE
Registered company number: 872828

www.pearsonschools.co.uk

First published by Pearson
a division of Pearson New Zealand Ltd
67 Apollo Drive, Rosedale, North Shore 0632, New Zealand
Associated companies throughout the world

Typesetting: Ruby-Anne Fenning
Front Cover Design: Lucy Hutchings
Back Cover Design: Ruby-Anne Fenning
Illustrations: Stu Duval

The right of Stu Duval to be identified as author of this work has been asserted by
him in accordance with the Copyright, Designs and Patents Act 1988.

First published 2011
This edition published 2012

2024
11

**British Library Cataloguing in Publication Data**
A catalogue record for this book is available from the British Library

ISBN 978-0-43507-596-5

**Copyright notice**

Printed in Great Britain

**Acknowledgements**
We would like to thank the children and teachers of Bangor Central Integrated Primary
School, NI; Bishop Henderson C of E Primary School, Somerset; Brookside Community
Primary School, Somerset; Cheddington Combined School, Buckinghamshire; Cofton
Primary School, Birmingham; Dair House Independent School, Buckinghamshire; Deal
Parochial School, Kent; Lawthorn Primary School, North Ayrshire; Newbold Riverside
Primary School, Rugby and Windmill Primary School, Oxford for their invaluable help in
the development and trialling of the Bug Club resources.

Every effort has been made to contact copyright holders of material reproduced in
this book. Any omissions will be rectified in subsequent printings if notice is given
to the publishers.

A division of Pearson New Zealand Ltd

# CONTENTS

# CHAPTER 1
## TERRIFIED JANE

5

Tam Spratley is my name. I was the cabin boy on the pirate ship *Terrified Jane*. I am only ten years of age, but I have seen things that would make you scream in the night.

I was orphaned as a small boy. My parents, God bless their memory, died of the plague and I was left adrift in the gutters and streets of Portsmouth. Until, one stormy day, fate led me to the docks and up the gangplank of this pirate ship.

Of course, I had no idea she was a pirate vessel then. Pirates and their ships are banned from every port on the English coast. The ship I found myself on was called the *Lucky Lou*. That is, until we put to sea. Then her Union Jack flag was lowered and the skull and crossbones hoisted in its place. She became the dreaded pirate ship *Terrified Jane*.

For two years, I knew no other home. The life of a cabin boy is not a fancy one. It's hard work from sun up to sun down. I slept in a rough hammock below decks. The air was foul down there. It was breathed by a crew of stinking pirates who had never seen a bar of soap and thought one bath a year was a wasted luxury! The food was foul and most often rotten, yet it was hot and filling in its own way.

But it was not the horrid food and hard work that filled me with fear. It was our captain – Ezekiel Tombs. Just saying his name gives me the shivers. There were those who were frightened of his very shadow and, standing at over seven feet tall, he cast a long one. His black moustache was as sharp as a stingray's tail. His single eye would burn into your soul like a fiery cannon ball.

Part of my job as cabin

boy was to serve him at his table. Being the captain, he ate by himself in his grand cabin. I can tell you, my hands would shake with fear when I poured his wine.

Even more frightening was the "pet" he kept in a wire cage on his tabletop. Most pirate captains would keep a parrot or a dog for company. Not Ezekiel Tombs. His pet was a terrifying black scorpion that he called "Virus".

Often, at the end of a meal, he would unlock Virus's cage. Then the hideous creature would scuttle over the dirty dishes, nibbling at the scraps. I had to be nimble to avoid the deadly stinger at the end of her terrible tail.

For this reason, serving at the captain's table each evening filled me with dread.

One night, while I was clearing the plates and avoiding Virus, Captain Tombs suddenly spoke to me. "Boy! What do you hear?"

I was stunned. He never talked to me at all. "W … what do you mean, Captain?" I mumbled back.

His single eye was glowing now. He thumped the table. "I mean what I say! What do you hear, boy?"

I was shaking with fear. "I … I don't hear anything, sir."

He slammed his fist on the table again. The forks and glasses jumped. Virus scuttled back to her cage.

"What do you hear below decks, boy?" he shouted. "I want to know what the crew is talking about!"

I gulped. Below decks, the crew were always talking about the captain. Whispers, curses, tittle-tattle, none of which I would dare repeat to him. The truth was, they feared him greatly and hated him more.

"Treasure, sir … They talk about treasure," I said quickly.

This was, of course, true. All pirates talk of treasure and the pirates on board *Terrified Jane* had reason to talk of treasure. They had not actually seen any treasure in more than two years!

"Treasure?" repeated the captain with a grim smile.

"Yes, sir, they talk of that all the time."

"And do they know where to find this treasure?"

I was sweating with fear now. "Ah, no, sir, they trust that only you would know such a thing, Captain."

He laughed out loud – a laugh like chains rattling. Then, suddenly, he stopped. He grabbed me by the collar and stuck his face close to mine. I could smell his hot, fetid breath. "I know where the gold is, boy. More gold than you have seen in your dreams! So close I can smell it. So close …"

I was terrified. Why was he telling me?

Then he let me go. I tumbled to the deck, then got up and scurried away as fast as I could.

"You tell the crew what I said, boy!" he called after me. "You tell them that only I know where the gold is!"

I raced out the cabin door, my heart pounding. Looking back one last time, I saw him stroking the back of his hideous pet. "I am still the captain of this ship, Virus," he was saying. "If anyone dares to speak against me, they know where they will rot!"

I knew the place he spoke of. The place all pirates feared the most. A place of nightmares. A place of death.

Rat Island.

# CHAPTER 2
## A LOOSE CANNON BALL

Poor Jimmy Tarbottom should have heeded the captain's warning. I liked Jimmy Tarbottom, but he talked too much and he talked too loudly. A pirate should always know when to shut up. Jimmy Tarbottom did not.

"Captain Ezekiel Tombs don't know where he's going," said Jimmy. "He don't know where to lay his hands on treasure.

"I know where to sail the *Terrified Jane* to find gold," boasted Jimmy. "Maybe I should be the new captain?"

I tried to tell him to be careful about what he said, but he wouldn't listen. Then, one day, when the sky was as black as the inside of a coffin, the captain called all the crew together.

We lined up nervously before him. The captain picked up a cannon ball. He stroked it like a black cat. "I love the feel of this here cannon ball," he said. "It reminds me of you, my crew."

We all looked at each other, wondering what he meant.

"A cannon ball doesn't ask questions or give advice," he continued. "It goes wherever the captain sends it. It does what it's told."

He began to move through the fearful crew, still carrying that black cannon ball, until he stopped beside Jimmy Tarbottom. Jimmy's eyes were wide with dread.

"Hold this for me, will you, Jimmy?" said the captain.

Jimmy took the ball in his shaking hands.

The captain leaned in close to Jimmy's face. A wicked smile spread over his lips. "Are you like this cannon ball, Jimmy?" he asked.

Jimmy spluttered. "I … t … try t … to be, sir," he stammered.

The captain's smile disappeared like fog

on a sunny morning. "No, Jimmy. Word around ship says you are a loose cannon ball."

"No, sir! It isn't true!"

"Oh, I think it is. Word around the ship says that you want to be captain."

"No, sir! It was just my big mouth …"

The captain twirled around to the crew. "I have decided to give Jimmy Tarbottom his wish!" he shouted.

We were all stunned, I can tell you, and so was Jimmy.

"He wants to be in charge, to be captain of his own crew," continued the captain. "So I have granted his wish."

Then Captain Ezekiel Tombs pointed out over the side of the boat. "Look!" he cried. "There is Jimmy Tarbottom's ship and crew!"

We all stared out to sea, where mist and black clouds swirled. Suddenly, out of the misty murk, a shape emerged. But it was no ship. It was an island – skull-shaped and rocky.

Jimmy's eyes bulged. I gasped in horror. The crew were as white as a ghost's laundry. It was Rat Island!

The last time I saw Jimmy Tarbottom, he was standing on the beach at Rat Island. The cannon ball was at his feet. He was crying out to us, "Don't leave me here! Not here!" His voice disappeared into the fog as we sailed away.

I had no idea what terrible things awaited Jimmy on Rat Island. But I could imagine.

That night, down below decks, I talked to Old Two Fingers. He was the oldest pirate on the *Terrified Jane*. He'd lost all his fingers but two while wrestling an octopus. The octopus had swallowed Two Fingers' share of some pirate loot – a bag of gold coins – and he wanted it back. He'd stuck his hands down that beast's throat. When he pulled them free, he left eight of his fingers behind.

Two Fingers knew all about Rat Island.

"So what kind of place is it?" I asked.

"A place you never want to go!"

"Have you been there?" I asked.

"Only once. But that was more than enough. I'm lucky to be alive."

"Who lives on the island?"

Two Fingers stared into a flickering candle. "No one lives there … not for long anyway. Just them cursed beasts."

"What beasts?"

"Rats! There are thousands of them, boy, swarming, crawling, gnawing …"

I felt a shiver go up my back. It was midnight. Outside the porthole, the sea and the sky were as black as each other. Somewhere out there was poor Jimmy Tarbottom, on Rat Island.

Suddenly, the captain's voice could be heard. "Cabin boy Spratley! Cabin boy Spratley! Get yourself up here or I'll have your guts for garters."

Why was the captain calling me at midnight? I had no idea what he wanted.

"Better hurry, boy!" said Old Two Fingers.

I scampered up the steps and approached the captain's cabin. I had never been so frightened in my life!

# CHAPTER 3
## A QUESTION OF TRUST

Captain Tombs was seated in the corner of his cabin. A black spider in a web.

His long legs stuck out from the chair and I saw his cutlass lying at his feet. An old map, wrinkled with age, lay over his lap. His large head was slumped on his chest and I thought he must be asleep.

My heart was beating like a drum. Should I wake him or should I tiptoe away? Either way, I'd no doubt get a tongue-lashing, maybe worse …

Suddenly, Captain Tombs spoke. Without moving his head from his chest, he hissed, "Lock the door, lad, and come closer."

With shaking hands, I bolted the cabin door and approached

him. Beneath my feet, the deck timbers creaked. The *Terrified Jane* rolled with every slap of the waves.

A single candle leaked its pus-yellow light over the table near the captain's seat. By its light, I caught a glimpse of the map sprawled on his lap. I wasn't much of a reader. I'd never been taught my letters, but I could read the words on that map well enough …

Rat Island!

The captain sat bolt upright and grabbed me by the wrist. "I see fear in your eyes, boy. I can smell it on you. What frightens you so?"

I tried to pull back, but his grip was an iron shackle around my wrist.

"Rat Island, sir!" I cried. "I saw your map …"

He released me with a sneering laugh. "You are right to fear it, lad. The Devil Himself fears that place. It crawls with vermin. They are so thick on the ground they climb upon each other's backs to get to you. They are so hungry they even eat each other!"

A picture of poor Jimmy Tarbottom sprang into my mind. I shuddered at the thought of him trapped on that hideous island, surrounded by hungry rats.

When Captain Tombs got to his feet, his head almost touched the cabin roof. He rolled up the map of Rat Island and stuffed it in his jacket pocket. Then he turned to face me. Yellow candlelight danced in his single eye.

"Are you a boy to be trusted, Tam Spratley?" he hissed.

I blinked at the question. It was so like the one he had asked of Jimmy Tarbottom! I tried to answer, but the words tumbled over my lips like a bucket of spilled spuds. "I … I … am a boy I trust … I mean, I am a trusty boy, sir."

He laughed at my clumsy reply. Then his eyes narrowed. "We shall see, young Spratley. There are others aboard this ship who do not know the meaning of trust. Do you know who I'm speaking of?"

"Jimmy Tarbottom, sir?"

He spat upon the floor. "Ha! He's but one of many. The decks below me crawl with untrustworthy snakes. Two Fingers ... the whole crew. Snakes, all of them!"

He reached down and snatched up his cutlass. Then, with a vicious swipe, he plunged the blade into the tabletop!

I was terrified. There was a madness in Captain Tombs' eye I had not seen before. Maybe I would be the next target for his blade. Then, just as suddenly as it came, his foul temper passed. He slumped back into his chair and beckoned me to sit. I was glad of a seat, for my own legs were weak with fear.

The captain reached into his pocket and, to my astonishment, produced a large golden coin. Holding it to the candlelight, he turned it in his long fingers. It twinkled in the dancing flame. "Have you ever seen one of these before, boy?" he asked.

"No, sir, indeed I have not … but I have dreamt of such."

He laughed. "It is what every pirate would sell his very mother for."

And then, to my utter amazement, he pressed the gold coin into the palm of my hand! "It is yours now, cabin boy," he said with a sly smile.

The coin burned into my palm like fire. "But, sir … why? What have I done to earn such a gift?"

"It is no gift, for you have yet to earn it. But you will."

"I don't understand …" I muttered, still staring at the coin.

He drew his face so close to mine I smelt his foul breath. "How many eyes do you see upon my face?"

"Just the one, sir," I replied, blinking in astonishment.

"Yes! And you, Tam Spratley, will be my other. You will go back below decks, to that pit of snakes, and you will be my eyes and my ears. I want to know what they whisper about me! What mutiny they plan against me! You will inform me at my table every evening."

I was stunned. So that was the reason for the midnight summons. I was to be a snitch, a sneak … a rat. And I could do nothing about it. To refuse the captain was unthinkable.

"Tell them nothing of our conversation or of the coin in your keeping. If they discover it, they will tear you to shreds and feed you to the sharks, just to get their hands on it!"

Then he laughed a dreadful laugh. "And, if I find you to be untrustworthy, boy, I will do the same."

# CHAPTER 4
## FIND THE MAP!

It was still pitch-black, hours before dawn, when I woke with a start. Someone was jabbing my ribs with a bony finger.

"Wake up, lad!" It was Old Two Fingers.

Below decks, there was the usual rumble of snores and the stench of unwashed pirates. I was used to that, but I had barely slept a wink. My mind had been tormented by the strange summons to Captain Tombs' cabin.

Two Fingers beckoned me to get up and follow him. I eased myself over the edge of my hammock, careful not to step on the face of the snoring pirate below me.

Suddenly, I remembered the gold coin. I had stashed it in the bottom of my shoe. Was it still there? Had Two Fingers found it?

"C'mon, lad. Before the whole ship wakes," he whispered, and he led the way up the wooden steps to the top deck.

I slid into my shoes and felt the cold edge of the coin. At least my terrible secret was safe … for the moment.

But what was Two Fingers up to?

The top deck was silent and black. The only sound was the groan and creak of the ship's timbers and the slosh of the waves. A cold breeze nipped at my ears like a hungry terrier.

Up on the foredeck, a light suddenly flared. Captain Tombs! No, it was only the keeper of the watch, lighting his pipe.

Two Fingers motioned me into the shelter of the giant mast. "I'll get straight to it, lad," he whispered, rubbing his damaged hands for warmth. "Spit it out. What was it that the captain wanted you for last night?"

Now my head was really spinning. Two Fingers had always been like a father to me. It was he who had taken me under his wing and found me work on the *Terrified Jane*. I had never kept a secret from him … until now.

"What's wrong with you, lad? You look like you've seen the Devil Himself," he said, searching my fearful eyes.

"Captain Tombs needed his boots shining," I lied, cursing myself for doing so.

"His boots? At midnight … in the middle of the ocean?" he asked suspiciously.

"You always said the captain was as mad as a sack of eels," I replied, trying to laugh. It sounded more like a dead man coughing.

"He talked of nothing else then?"

"Nothing."

"Did he have any maps lying about, lad? Think carefully now."

"No. Not a thing. His table was as bare as a poor man's pantry."

Two Fingers rubbed his bristly chin. "He's up to something, lad. I can smell it in the air … It's a rotten smell, to be sure!"

I said nothing, but I peered over my shoulder toward the captain's dark cabin windows.

"I have sailed with him for thirty years," continued Two Fingers. "Through storms and seas that'd make a cannon ball weep.

He's flogged us, threatened us, marooned us – more times than I can remember. But he always knew where the treasure was buried.

"We filled our pockets with loot in them days. That's why I've stuck with him all these years – but not now. We ain't seen treasure for two whole years! Two years without even a whiff of gold. The crew can't wait no longer … It's time to take matters into our own hands!"

I couldn't believe what I was hearing. "Mutiny?" I gasped. "Don't you remember what happened to poor Jimmy Tarbottom!"

Two Fingers spat on the deck. "Tarbottom was a loud-mouthed fool who got what he deserved!"

"Who else is with you?" I asked, still shocked at the very thought of mutiny.

"Jasper Maggot, Toothless Grin, Jamaican Bob – to name but a few. The whole crew is ready to mutiny. That just leaves you, lad. Will you join us, Tam? We need you for our plan to work."

I was shaking from head to foot. "You need *me* for your plan? What plan? What can I possibly do? I'm just a cabin boy!"

"Exactly!" hissed Two Fingers. "And what does a cabin boy do? Why, he spends time in the captain's cabin, of course. Serving him dinner, pouring his drinks, listening to his ramblings, watching where he hides his secrets."

"His secrets?"

"Aye. Somewhere in his cabin is a map. A treasure map. He guards it like an octopus guards its eggs. It ain't no use the crew taking over the ship if we don't first have that map!"

I gulped. "You want *me* to find it?"

"Yes, lad. Find it, steal it and bring it to me. Then I swear on my granny's grave you'll share in the loot."

"But what about Captain Tombs?"

I could just see Two Fingers' sneer in the darkness. "He'll be getting a taste of his own medicine. On Rat Island!"

He grabbed hold of my arm. "So, will you join us? Will you get the map, Tam?"

I felt sick to my stomach. What should I say? Somewhere in the darkness, I could feel Captain Tombs' one eye staring into my soul. The gold coin hidden in my shoe felt like a red-hot ember.

"Let me think about it," was all I could say.

Two Fingers' eyes opened wide with astonishment. Or was it suspicion?

"Very well, boy, you think about my offer – but I'll only give you till tomorrow at sunrise. Either you're with us, Tam, or you're against us. Remember that!"

He turned and shuffled off below decks. In the distance, the sky was turning blood-red with the sunrise. By this time tomorrow, I'd need to make a decision.

I ran to the side of the boat and vomited.

# CHAPTER 5
## A DAGGER IN MY BACK

A pirate ship is a small village. Nothing much is secret. Everyone knows everyone's business, and news travels as fast as the plague.

By the time I had headed back down the steps to my hammock, I could tell Old Two Fingers had spread the word. Jasper Maggot, who had the hammock below me, glared at me with a steely eye. Toothless Grin, whispering with Jamaican Bob, stopped his conversation to look daggers at me.

Hastily, I stowed my hammock and scurried off to my first chore of the day – helping Cook get breakfast ready.

The galley, on the lower deck, was small and cluttered, but I was glad of the warmth from the smoky oven, and glad to be away from the stares and glares of the crew.

The old cook was a deaf mute. He neither spoke nor heard a thing. This was useful, for Cook's food was the foulest, filthiest food ever slopped on a plate. The pirate crew might hoot and howl over every serving, but the old cook never heard a word. Even Captain Tombs' foul curses and threats fell on deaf ears.

Cook was stirring a bubbling black brew when I arrived. I shuddered to think what might be in it, but I could make a guess from the gory guts on the chopping board.

He signalled to me to take over the stirring. While I pushed and prodded at the nasty brew, I could hear the ship coming to life above me. Hammocks were stowed, sails trimmed, decks mopped, ropes lashed.

It was just another day aboard the *Terrified Jane*.

It was also the day I had to make a decision that could cost me my life. Join Two Fingers and the others or side with Captain Tombs?

One had paid me with gold, the other with friendship.

I looked around the galley. Cook had gone. Reaching into my shoe, I removed the gold coin. Why had I ever taken it? I could simply toss it overboard, but what if Captain Tombs suddenly demanded it back?

Or maybe I should just tell Two Fingers – show him the coin? Would he believe my story, though? Would the crew call me a traitor … a rat?

I stirred and stirred, lost in thought. Behind me, I heard the galley door close. Had Cook finally returned? I began to slosh the breakfast slop into bowls.

Suddenly, a hand grabbed my shoulder. Before I could turn to see who it was, I felt a sharp jab in my back.

"Easy now, lad," hissed a voice, "or this dagger might get stuck in your ribs!"

"Who are you? What do you want?" I gasped.

"The question is, who are you? And what do *you* want, lad?" hissed the voice.

I could not recognise it – but I did recognise the point of a dagger pricking my back!

"Why are you threatening me?" I demanded.

"Maybe it is you who threatens all of us," replied the voice.

"I've done nothing!"

"That's the truth," sneered the voice, "but you can no longer do nothing. Take sides! Do the thing that was asked of you by the mast this very morning!"

"And if I don't?" I said, with more bravery than I felt.

The dagger pressed harder against my skin. "Then you'll end up on Rat Island with Tombs!"

The dagger withdrew. The door slammed shut. I whirled around to catch sight of whoever it was, but they had disappeared into the bowels of the ship.

All that day I watched my back as I went about my tasks. I sloshed water over the decks and mopped them till they shone. I pumped filthy bilge water from the hold till my back ached. I sewed canvas patches on the torn sails till my fingers bled.

All day, the crew eyed me as if I had some disease, but no one approached me or threatened me. Only once did Old Two Fingers catch my eye. He gave me a smile, but his eyes were as cold as marbles.

Captain Tombs had not ventured from his cabin all day, but that was not unusual. Sometimes the crew didn't clap eyes on him for weeks at a time. Then he'd suddenly explode from his cabin – shouting orders, whipping the crew with his tongue.

But I knew for certain that I would be seeing him soon enough.

The sun had bled into the sea and night was leaking its black ink into the sky when, with a trembling hand, I took the dinner tray from Cook's galley. Up the wooden steps I went to Captain Tombs' cabin.

Along the top deck, the crew were lined up – black crows watching as I passed.

They said not a word, but I knew exactly what they wanted.

# CHAPTER 6
## A CLOSE ENCOUNTER

I knocked on the captain's door. There was no answer. I knocked again. Nothing.

The door was unlocked, so I gently pushed it open. Stepping inside, I looked about for the captain. He was nowhere to be seen.

A candle burned on his table, lighting up Virus's cage. The door was open, but there was no sign of the scorpion either.

I set the dinner tray carefully down on the table, keeping a watch out for the creature. And that's when I saw it – not the scorpion, but the map. It was lying on the bottom of Virus's cage.

So this is where Captain Tombs hides his precious map, I thought, my mind whirring. Glancing about, heart pounding, I checked again for any sign of him.

Maybe he was asleep. I listened for the sound of his snores, but heard nothing.

My eyes darted back to the map in the cage. This could be my opportunity. Take the map!

But that would be joining my fate to that of the crew. I'd be a mutineer. There could be no turning back.

Slowly, I reached out my hand. It was as if I were watching another person's arm, not my own. My fingers were upon it now, sliding it carefully out of the cage.

Suddenly, I caught a hint of movement, a blur of black. It was Virus! She had hidden herself under the map! So now I was drawing her closer with every pull.

I froze with fear. In a flash, the horrible creature leapt from the underside of the map right onto my bare arm, her stinger raised.

Paralysed with fear, I watched as she crawled – up, up, up. I felt her hideous feet, saw her black bejewelled eyes. Would I soon feel her vicious sting?

Then, out of the cabin's shadows, a figure emerged. Captain Ezekiel Tombs! In two lanky strides he was beside me. He must have been seated in the dark the whole time, watching me!

"Well, well," he purred, like a tom-cat with a mouse in its grasp. "If I were you, boy, I'd stay very still. My darling wee pet doesn't like thieves. Was the gold coin I paid you not enough? You take my gold and now you take my map?"

I could feel Virus crawling over my collar!

"Captain, sir!" I heard myself wail. "I did not mean to take your map!"

He leered at me, his hot breath by my left ear. "Then maybe it was my sweet Virus you were wanting to meet?"

"N … no, sir!" I cried, still frozen stiff as the creature climbed my neck.

"Well then, cabin boy, you have exactly one minute to tell me the truth, or Virus will climb across your face and strike your lying eyes."

I had no choice. "It's true!" I cried. "I was reaching for your map!"

"Why?" he demanded.

"I was forced to take it!"

"*Forced*? By whom?"

I could barely speak. Virus was crawling over my mouth. I did not want to betray my friend, but I was terrified … "Two Fingers," I mumbled through gritted teeth.

"Aha!" shouted the captain. "I knew it! I knew he'd be the one behind it all."

Virus was on my nose now, her stinger set to strike. Then, with a sudden scoop of his hand, Captain Tombs whisked the beast off my face and sent her scurrying back into her cage. He slammed the door shut and bolted it.

I felt the cabin spinning and collapsed to the floor. As I fell, my head caught the corner of the table. Blackness rose like a full tide in my brain. The last thing I saw was a shadowy face peering through the window. It was Two Fingers! He had seen and heard everything.

I do not know how long I was unconscious. My dreams were filled with scorpions. They had the head of Captain Tombs and Two Fingers sat at their tail. They were chasing me past a clutch of crows who screamed, "Get the map! Get the map!"

Muskets fired, cutlasses clanged, then rough hands grabbed at me. I felt as if I were being tossed overboard …

Suddenly, cold water was dashed in my face. My shoulder was being shaken violently.

"Wake up, boy! Open your eyes!"

Painfully, my eyes opened to an unbelievable sight. Captain Tombs was looming over me. He was bleeding from a wound in his shoulder. His clothes were ripped and torn.

I tried to get to my feet, but the deck suddenly rolled wildly.

"Sit down! Keep still or you'll capsize us both!" he cried.

"Capsize us?" I mumbled weakly. "How?"

"Take a look for yourself, boy," was all he said.

I looked. What I saw could not have filled me with more dread. I was in a rowboat. All around me was the empty ocean. I could see no sign of the *Terrified Jane* – and my only companion was Captain Ezekiel Tombs!

"Am I in some nightmare?" I whimpered.

"This is no dream, boy. We have been cast adrift."

"Adrift! By whom? Where is the crew? The ship?"

"Mutineers, all of them. May their teeth rot in their heads!"

Then he told me what had happened while I had lain unconscious. "The crew came a-knocking. It seems Old Two Fingers, curse his eyes, had planned to mutiny this very evening. When I refused to open my door, he blew it down with cannon fire and stormed my cabin!

"I put up a fearsome fight. But, in the end, I was overwhelmed by those rats. Still, I sent Toothless Grin and Jamaican Bob to Davy Jones' locker! Alas, my poor Virus went with them."

"And then what happened?" I asked, still barely able to believe my ears.

"Then they had themselves a pirates' court."

"A pirates' court?"

"Aye, lad. It's a court where they have already decided the verdict before the trial begins. In their eyes I was as guilty as sin. You, too, Tam Spratley."

"Guilty! Of what crime?"

"They found the coin I gave you, boy. Two Fingers testified that you were in my pay. They called you a filthy rat."

When I heard those words, I felt sick. I had been betrayed by my dearest friend.

"Then they ripped my cabin apart looking for the map," continued the captain.

"The treasure map? The one in Virus's cage?"

He let out a wicked laugh. "That map is worthless. You almost got yourself stung for a useless piece of paper, lad. Right now, the crew are sailing north by north-west, using a worthless map to find a treasure island that is as real as my missing eye. And they've left us in this leaky boat with neither food nor water!"

"Left alone to die on the ocean," I moaned.

The captain smiled a death's-head grin. "No, no. We are close to landfall."

"Landfall?" I shouted, hope springing to life at last. "Where, sir?"

He pointed a long, bony finger to the south and I turned eagerly to see where this land lay. There, on the distant horizon, lit up by the sunrise, was an island.

"Hooray!" I cried, tears of joy running down my cheeks. "What is that blessed island called, sir?"

"If I am not mistaken," said he, in a voice like a coffin lid closing, "it is called Rat Island."

# CHAPTER 8
## TARBOTTOM'S SOUVENIR

I never wanted to set foot on that cursed island. Captain Tombs had to drag me ashore by my arm.

I recognised the rocky bay we landed on immediately. It was the beach where I had last seen poor Jimmy Tarbottom. Back then I had been safely on board the *Terrified Jane*. Now I was stumbling up that same dreaded beach myself.

Suddenly, I tripped on something smooth and hard. It was a rusty cannon ball! Jimmy's cannon ball. I felt sick to my stomach.

A barking laugh came from up ahead. "Looks like Tarbottom left us a souvenir!" the captain called back over his shoulder.

"Where are we going?" I called.

"To higher ground!"

Still faint-headed from the blow to my head, I yelled at his tall, ragged back, "I will stay here and rest a while, sir!"

The captain whirled around and strode back down the rocks towards me.

"What do you see on this beach, boy?" he hissed when he reached me.

I looked up and down the narrow beach. "I see rocks, sand, driftwood and Jimmy's cannon ball."

He sneered. "Wrong, cabin boy. What you see is rocks, sand, Jimmy's cannon ball and *bones*!"

I looked again. Yes! What I had thought were piles of bleached driftwood were actually bones. Human bones!

I recoiled in horror. "Who has done this?" I cried.

"Not *who*. *What*." He leaned forward to hiss a single word in my ear. "*Rats*!" Then he strode away and disappeared into the fringe of black jungle.

I did not need to be told twice. In a flash, I was on my feet and rushing to join him.

For hours we crashed through that jungle. Vines like octopus tentacles reached out to grab us at every step. There was no path to follow, so Captain Tombs used his cutlass to hack a way forward.

I looked nervously from side to side as I went, certain that the rats were watching us.

By late afternoon, we had finally emerged from the steaming jungle. Before us was a steep, rocky hill. I slumped to the ground exhausted, for I had had no water to drink or food to eat since we were cast adrift.

"On your feet, lad," cried Captain Tombs, who seemed untroubled by hunger or thirst. "We have much work to do before night falls!"

"Work, sir?" I moaned

"We work or we die," he said, as he began to hack at a tree branch with his cutlass. "When night falls, the rats will attack. They will smell the blood from my wound like sharks in the sea."

I was horrified. "How will we defend ourselves?"

"With fire," he grunted, hacking at another branch. "Rats are afraid of fire. We build a ring of burning fire around us and stand our guard."

I leapt to help him, forgetting my thirst and hunger.

We finished just as darkness started to soak the sky. A heaped circle of branches was stacked around us. In the middle, we had stored another heap. We would need to keep the fire blazing all night.

Captain Tombs took a tinderbox from his pocket and struck the flint. Nothing happened. Again he struck the flint. Again no spark leapt to light our fire.

"It is still damp from the sea!" he cried.

Suddenly, I caught sight of something moving on the hill above. I peered up into the gloom. It seemed as if the whole hill was moving. I rubbed my eyes, thinking my mind was playing tricks on me.

Then a wave of sound rolled down the slope towards us. As long as I live, I will never forget that sound. It was a high-pitched squeal – a demon-like screech that turned my blood to ice.

I had heard such a terrifying sound once before, on the *Terrified Jane*. Down below decks, collecting a sack of flour for Cook, I had uncovered a rat's nest. A huge mother rat was cornered, raised up on her hind legs. She spat at me with such venom and made such a fearful screech that I backed away as fast as my legs would carry me.

But this sound, from the hill above, was a thousand times worse.

Captain Tombs spun around. "It's the rats, boy!"

The earth seemed to explode. A wave of rats was pouring down towards us like black lava!

"Light the fire, Captain!" I screamed

Again and again he tried, but no spark came. The rats were almost upon us now.

"You light the flame, boy!" he shouted, tossing me the flint. "I'll hold the beasts back as long as I can!"

He leapt over the firewood, swinging his cutlass, taking the lead rats by surprise. He waded into them, hacking about him with huge blows. Their squeals of pain and rage were terrible to hear.

My fingers shook with fear as I tried to strike a spark.

"Hurry, boy! I can't hold them off much longer!" cried the captain.

I had almost given up hope when a spark leapt from my flint and ignited the dry branches. Within seconds, dancing orange flames were roaring up in a circle of fire.

The captain leapt back over the fiery barricade, dead rats still clinging to his boots.

Through the fire we could see the rats turning back in the face of the flames. Their red eyes glowed angrily.

"Back, you beasts!" cried Captain Tombs. "Back to your rat holes! You'll not dine on us this night!"

We kept watch through the night. Dark shapes scuttled in the shadows beyond the firelight, but no rat dared cross the barricade of flame.

At some point I must have fallen asleep because, when I woke, the fire was burning low. I sprang up to stoke it, and that's when I realised that Captain Tombs was nowhere to be seen!

I called his name but he did not answer. Maybe he has gone to collect more wood, I thought. I waited till dawn, and still he did not return.

There was no movement on the hill. The

rats had gone back to their holes.

By mid morning, I felt it was safe enough to leave my fire circle and set out to find Captain Tombs.

# CHAPTER 9
## DARK PLACES

The sun was as hot as a branding iron when I began the climb the hill, hoping I might be able to spot the captain from the top.

The climb was steep and treacherous, with sheer drops threatening on all sides. I passed many narrow tunnels and caves set into the hillside. The entrances were just big enough for a small dog to crawl through. I shuddered to think what lay inside those dark places. Judging from the bones at the entrances, I could guess!

The hill itself seemed to be made of razor-sharp lava rock. So, by the time I finally reached the top, I was covered with cuts and scratches.

From up there the view was amazing. I could see the whole island. To the south lay dark jungle and the rocky bay where we had landed. East and west were bogs and swamp, unfit for human or rat.

The north was more interesting. In that direction, a gentle slope ran down from the hill and entered a forest of palm trees. Beyond that, I caught a glimpse of a wide sandy bay. Running through the palms to the bay was a sight that cheered my heart. A stream! Sparkling in the hot sun.

Maybe that was the reason for Captain Tombs' mysterious disappearance? He went looking for water.

I scrambled down the hill and sprinted through the palms to the stream. Without even taking off my shoes, I dived head-first into a crystal pool. Oh, the joy of that cool water! I drank my fill and splashed about as happily as a pig in mud.

For a moment, I forgot all about the *Terrified Jane*, the mutineers, Captain Tombs and the rats. I was alive and free.

I felt nothing could surprise me now.

But I was wrong for, as I climbed out of the stream, I saw a figure standing in the shadows … Captain Ezekiel Tombs.

"Come, boy," he said. "I've got something to show you."

I should have been glad to see him. I didn't want to spend another night battling the rats alone. But something about his manner troubled me deeply.

I followed him through the palms to the sandy bay beyond. "What is it you wish to show me, sir?" I asked, for the bay was empty.

He laughed a cruel laugh and, pointing out to sea, said, "I thought you might like to see an old friend."

I squinted in the bright sun, but could see nothing. Then, suddenly, a dark shape came into view. Against the sun, all I could see was a black silhouette, but I would have recognised that shape anywhere. It was the *Terrified Jane*!

"Have they come back to hunt us?" I cried

in alarm.

"No, there is something else to be hunted!" crowed the captain harshly.

I had no idea what he was talking about. I turned to watch in alarm as the ship dropped anchor and a rowboat began to make its way to shore. To my surprise, there seemed to be only one person in the boat – Old Two Fingers!

Now my heart was racing. Where was the crew? I scanned the ship. There wasn't a single pirate to be seen. The deck looked empty, the masts the same.

It was as if the *Terrified Jane* had become a ghost ship.

Two Fingers leapt out of the boat and dragged it up the sandy beach. I expected Captain Tombs to draw his cutlass and charge down to the water to fight him. Yet, to my surprise, he raised a hand as if he were greeting a long-lost shipmate!

"Avast, Two Fingers! What took you so

long!" he shouted in a joking tone.

"Avast, Captain!" replied Two Fingers. "I had to lose some unwanted baggage first."

They both laughed gleefully at this. Then Two Fingers spotted me. "I see you've got the lad in tow," he said.

"Aye," replied the captain, "though it's been no easy chore taking care of him. Like having a useless dog on a lead!"

"Well, he'll be of use tonight," grunted Two Fingers, suddenly grim.

I had no idea what they were talking about. My mind spun like a dropped coin, trying to make sense of it all.

"W … Where's the crew?" I quavered.

Two Fingers chuckled evilly. "The crew? I left them sitting on a desert island beach, slowly dying of thirst with only a useless treasure map to eat!"

For a moment, he and the captain were doubled over with laughter at this thought.

"Don't you see it, lad?" sneered Two

Fingers when he saw my confusion. "This has all been planned."

"Planned? By who?"

"Me and the captain here."

I turned to Captain Tombs. "You? *And him*? W … Why?" I stammered.

"Treasure, boy, *treasure*!"

My eyes opened wide with shock. Suddenly, I could see the whole thing for what it was. A plan, a trick, and I had been completely blind to it. What a fool I'd been! "The treasure is here on Rat Island," I gasped.

They nodded.

"Then why didn't you simply sail here years ago and dig it up?"

"Then we'd have had to share it with a crew of other pirates," replied Two Fingers.

"And now we only have to divide by two," added Captain Tombs, with a nasty laugh.

A sudden chill ran up my spine. "Then why do you need me? Why am I here?"

The captain grabbed me by the arm. "We

need you, lad, because the treasure isn't exactly buried."

"Not buried?" I asked, squirming in his grip. "Then where?"

Two Fingers grabbed my other arm roughly. "In a cave," he croaked. "And the only way to get to that cave is through a tunnel – a rather *narrow* tunnel."

I recalled the dark, narrow tunnels in the side of the rocky hill and shivered. So that was it. *They* couldn't get to the treasure. Tombs was far too tall and Old  Two Fingers' hands were useless for digging.

So I had been chosen to do their dirty work. How long had they been planning this, I wondered?

As if reading my mind, the captain took up the story.

"Thirty years ago, Two Fingers and I were crew on a pirate ship, the *Hangman's Noose*. The captain was a cunning brute named Geraldo Creep. He seized a Spanish ship laden with a king's ransom of gold and jewels – and he had the clever idea of burying it deep in the tunnels of this very island."

"But what of the rats?" I asked

"There were no rats then," he said. "A cabin boy, such as yourself, was used to crawl down the narrowest tunnels and convey the treasure to a secret cave. All went well, except for the one thing Captain Creep had not planned on. The plague! It swept through the crew of the *Hangman's Noose*, killing all but me and Two Fingers.

"We had to bury them all on the beach, including Geraldo Creep. Then we set fire to that plague ship and rowed away. That's how the rats came. They escaped the flaming ship and swarmed ashore.

"Over the years, they've grown in numbers beyond imagining! All that long time we two have waited and watched. Nobody would dare venture onto an island of rats, so we knew the treasure would be safe. All we needed was someone to crawl down those tunnels and get the treasure for us. I sent Two Fingers ashore two years ago to find a suitable lad. A small, skinny lad, I said – and he came back with you, Tam Spratley!"

I felt sick. All these years I had thought of Two Fingers as a father, saving me from the gutter and giving me a place to call home, but now it turned out it was all part of a plan. I was chosen the way a rabbit hunter chooses a skinny dog – to go down holes!

"So the mutiny was all a hoax?"

Two Fingers grinned at the thought of his own cunning. "We needed the stupid crew to think you were the captain's snitch. Then, when I stirred up the mutiny, they willingly agreed to cast you both adrift."

"We had to have you for the tunnels," snarled Captain Tombs.

I was still stunned at all I had heard. Then another thought hit me like a cannon broadside. "But those tunnels are full of rats! They'll tear anyone who goes down there to pieces. What makes you think I will ever agree to go down there?"

"You will do what you are ordered to do, boy!" shouted the captain. He drew his cutlass as Two Fingers bound my hands behind me.

"Tonight we will lead you to the entrance of the treasure tunnel," he hissed in my ear. "Then the captain and I will lead those rats away to the south of the island. You'll have a short time only to get down that hole and bring us back all of Geraldo Creep's treasure. If you know what's good for you, boy, you'll do as we say." He twisted my ear painfully and I felt Captain Tombs' cutlass in my back. What choice did I have?

I watched the sun set, sinking into the ocean like a drowning man. Darkness would soon cloak Rat Island, and soon I would have to crawl through those hideous tunnels!

I was still bound to a palm tree on the beach, but it wasn't long before Captain Tombs arrived to untie my wrists. Any thoughts of freedom were soon proved wrong, however. He carried with him a huge length of chain, which he bolted around my waist. Then, without a word, he began pulling me by the chain up the track to the hill of rats.

We climbed almost to the summit, the island fast turning black below us. Finally, we arrived at the cave entrance. The stench of rats was everywhere. A huge thorn bush, with a trunk as thick as a man's arm, grew by the entrance. Around this trunk, the captain bolted the other end of the chain.

I felt like a dog on a lead.

"This is the tunnel, boy," he said, pointing into the blackness.

"What about the rats?" I asked nervously.

He smiled wickedly in the dark, his teeth glowing like those in a skull's head. "Two Fingers has prepared them a little treat. Can't you smell it, boy?"

Suddenly, my nostrils flared and I gagged violently. Wafting up the hill was a stench so vile it turned my stomach.

"What is that stink?"

"It's a barrel of Cook's fish guts, octopus lungs and intestines, left for the sun to ripen and rot. Once the rats get a whiff of that lot, they'll be driven crazy with hunger. Never fear, boy, they'll ignore you altogether in their rush to get to that stinking barrel!"

I prayed he was correct.

From the base of the hill, Two Fingers' voice could be heard. "Come on, Captain! It's dinner time for them little vermin beasties!"

"When the rats have eaten the offal, they'll come for you," I said, trying to sound braver than I felt. "Where will you hide?"

"Same as last night," said the captain with a shrug. "We have a circle of dry wood ready to fire. Two Fingers and I will stay there till you have the gold."

"How will I get the gold back up the tunnel?"

"The tunnel will be too narrow for you to drag up the largest chests, so you'll have to bring it up an armful at a time. It'll be dark down there, with many turns in the tunnel, but the chain will guide you back. Don't delay, boy! We can't keep them rats at bay with our trickery for long!"

He could feel my fear, I'm sure, for he laid a hand on my head then. "Bring us Geraldo Creep's gold, boy, and I swear I'll give you a portion and set you free."

Then he was gone into the darkness.

I didn't believe a word he said. And I had never felt so alone in all my life.

The moon was rising fast. So was the stench from Cook's horrible barrel of guts. Suddenly, the ground beneath my feet began to shake. I clutched at the chain in fear.

Then came a sound like ten thousand claws scratching a giant blackboard. The rats were coming! Thousands of red eyes stabbed through the dark as they poured out of the caves in a tsunami of black fur.

Tumbling, clawing, screeching, they teemed down the hillside, spilling over me like a filthy black blanket. I huddled in a ball, waiting for a thousand teeth to tear at my flesh. Then, wonder of wonders, the sound of their hisses and squeals disappeared down the hill.

The captain's plan had worked. Intoxicated by the stench of offal, they had left me alone. Now was my chance. I clenched my teeth and plunged into the cave.

The cave narrowed almost immediately. I cracked my head on the rocky roof and felt a trickle of blood. Soon I was forced to scrabble on my hands and knees, dragging the chain behind me.

Down and down I plunged, until I began to feel like a filthy rat myself. Then, after an hour of crawling, I came to a dead end. Desperately, I clawed at the walls of the tunnel for a way forward. There was none! I was trapped ... like a rat.

I scrunched my legs up to my chest and wept in frustration and fear.

# CHAPTER 10
## THE CAVERN OF RICHES

Then I heard it – a faint sound coming from the rocky wall behind me!

I listened in the darkness. There it was again. It sounded like metal on rock, as if someone were chinking away with a steel tool. Suddenly, the rock wall at my back cracked and splintered. I ducked as fragments of stone came flying through the dark. Now a shaft of yellow light was glinting through the crack.

Another blow sounded and, to my amazement, the head of a pickaxe broke through the rock! Soon there was a hole big enough for me to crawl through. A long arm reached out to help me.

I blinked in the sudden bright light. On the other side was a huge cavern. Candles lit the walls and in their golden glow I could see, for the first time, who had helped me.

I could have died of shock. It was none other than Jimmy Tarbottom!

Seeing Jimmy again left me speechless,

and the sight of what lay beyond him made my head spin. Glinting and sparkling in the candlelight was Captain Geraldo Creep's treasure!

There must have been twenty chests of gold and jewels spilt out on the cavern floor. Before me lay pearl necklaces, diamonds, rubies and emeralds, silver sovereigns and gold ducats – a king's ransom indeed.

I could barely tear my eyes away from the glittering trove to Jimmy Tarbottom. He was seated, grinning, on a wooden treasure chest. He offered me a swig of water from a golden cup and told me his tale.

"The first night on the island," he said, "I thought I would surely die. At dark, the rats came for me on the beach where I was marooned. But Fate took pity on me. I saw a little rock out in the bay, just big enough for a man to stand on. So, with the rats pouring down the beach, I swam for my life to that rock.

"There I spent a desperate night, clinging on till dawn. The rats could not swim out to me. At sunrise, they all vanished back to their holes and I swam ashore and explored the island. I discovered the rats' hill, their tunnels and the beach on the northern side. Each day, I would forage for food – coconut and fish. Then, at nightfall, I would swim back to my rock in the bay.

"It was on one of my daily explorations that I stumbled on a hidden tunnel that did not reek of rats. I followed it as far as I could, digging like a mole in places. I thought it might lead me to a safe shelter, away from the rats. What I found instead was this treasure!"

"What of the rats though?" I asked. "Don't they come back here at dawn?"

"No," replied Jimmy. "They don't seem to use this tunnel. They've no use for gold, I suppose. This cavern has only one entrance anyway, and I seal that up each night."

He smiled a grim smile. "So, here I was,

with a fortune in gold and jewels, stuck on Rat Island with no hope of escape. That was until this very night, when I  found you crawling in my tunnels. Were you marooned like me, Tam Spratley?"

Quickly, I told him my story. I told of Captain Tombs and Two Fingers' treacherous plan and how I had been fooled. I told of how the crew had been tricked and left to starve on a desert island. "And soon Tombs will tug on my chain, as if I were a dog. Then I will have to take this treasure back to the surface," I finished gloomily.

By now, Jimmy Tarbottom was laughing out loud.

"What do you find so funny, Jimmy?" I demanded.

"I am laughing at our good fortune, cabin boy Spratley!" he said, chuckling.

"You call this good fortune? To be trapped in a cavern of riches, surrounded by savage rats, with Tombs and Two Fingers waiting for us above!"

"They may wait," said Jimmy, "but they'll wait in vain. We'll be far away from this stinking island before the dawn!"

"How exactly?"

"On the *Terrified Jane*, you fool!" he said, with a slightly crazy laugh. "The ship at anchor in the bay awaits its two new captains, Tarbottom and Spratley."

"But what of Tombs and Two Fingers? They'll never let this treasure out of their grasp!"

"They will have their hands full with the rats," replied Jimmy, with a grim chuckle. "In the meantime, we must rid you of that chain and start carrying this loot to the beach. I'll show you the way."

So we both toiled long into the night, dragging Captain Geraldo Creep's treasure through Jimmy Tarbottom's tunnel to the bay. When the chests were finally stacked on the beach, he turned to me. "Row these out to the ship, Tam. I'm off to see what Tombs and Two Fingers are up to."

Then he disappeared into the night.

By dawn's first flush I was exhausted. All the chests had been safely rowed out to the *Terrified Jane* and stowed below. Now I waited nervously on the ship's prow, looking out for any sign of Jimmy or, worse, Captain Tombs and Two Fingers.

I half expected them to come charging down the bay, angry as mad dogs. By the time the sun had risen hot above the bay, however, the beach was still empty.

Suddenly, a figure emerged, running through the palms. It was Jimmy! He dived into the water and swam with strong strokes towards the *Terrified Jane*. I went down to the stern to help haul him up over the side.

"Are Captain Tombs and Two Fingers following?" I asked, staring back over the bay.

He lay gasping on the deck like a hooked fish, getting his breath back.

"No. They won't be doing any more chasing."

When his breath was fully restored, he told me what had happened.

"While you were stashing the loot, I sneaked back to the jungle. I followed the foul smell of the offal barrel. I found Tombs and Two Fingers laying a trail of that disgusting bait. The rats were following them in a feeding frenzy. Then I crept ahead of the two of them and found their circle of firewood."

"What did you do, Jimmy?" I asked, wide-eyed at his courage. "Did you fight them hand to hand?"

"No, lad, not with a blade or a musket, but with water!"

"Water?" I cried in disbelief.

"Yes! I poured water over their dry firewood. When it was soaked, I hid to watch. They soon came running. The rats were hard on their heels, for all the offal was devoured. Tombs and Two Fingers leapt into their circle of firewood and tried to set it alight, but, alas, it would not burn. In vain they tried. And soon the rats came swarming over the wet wood …"

His voice trailed away and we both looked back at Rat Island, imagining the terrible scene. I shuddered.

"Come on, cabin boy," said Jimmy Tarbottom, getting to his feet. "We have a ship to sail and a treasure to spend!"

"Where will we sail?"

"First, we rescue the crew from their desert island. They'll be even happier to see us when they clap eyes on the loot below decks!"

"And then?"

"We sail for a place that has everything we need – everything except one thing."

"What might that be?" I asked

He laughed out loud.

"Rats, Tam Spratley. *Rats*!"